Cinema is a fragile medium. Many of the great classic films of the past

which ''' is a base operated regularly at the last seum of the Moving
Image in London in a year-round repertory.

BFI Publishing has now commissioned a series of books to stand
alongside these titles. Authors, including film critics and scholars,
film-makers, novelists, historians and those distinguished in the arts,
have been invited to write on a film of their choice, drawn from the
Archive's list. Each volume will present the author's own insights into
the chosen film, together with a brief production history and a detailed
filmography, notes and bibliography. The numerous illustrations have
been specially made from the Archive's own prints.

With new titles published each year, the BFI Film Classics series
will rapidly grow into an authoritative and highly readable guide to the
great films of world cinema.

Poster for *The Seventh Seal*

BFI FILM

CLASSICS

THE SEVENTH SEAL
(DET SJUNDE INSEGLET)

....

Melvyn Bragg

BFI PUBLISHING

First published in 1993 by the
BRITISH FILM INSTITUTE
21 Stephen Street, London W1P 1PL

British Library Cataloguing in Publication Data

Bragg, Melvyn
    The Seventh Seal – (Film Classics Series)
    I. Title   II. Series
    791.43

    ISBN 0–85170–391–7

Designed by
Andrew Barron & Collis Clements Associates

Typesetting by
Fakenham Photosetting Limited, Norfolk

Printed in Great Britain by
The Trinity Press, Worcester

CONTENTS

· ·

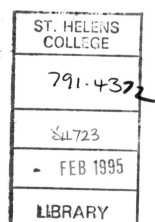

To Michael Wolfers
for the Cherwell *years*

ACKNOWLEDGMENTS

Stills are from the Stills, Posters and Design Department of the British Film Institute and from the Swedish Film Institute. The credits were checked by Markku Salmi.

Bergman on the set of *The Seventh Seal*

1
. . . .
ART AND RELIGION

Regardless of my own beliefs and my own doubts, which are
unimportant in this connection, it is my opinion that art lost its
basic creative drive the moment it was separated from worship. It
severed an umbilical cord and now lives its own sterile life,
generating and degenerating itself. In former days the artist
remained unknown and his work was to the glory of God. He
lived and died without being more or less important than other
artisans; 'eternal values', 'immortality' and 'masterpiece' were
terms not applicable in his case. The ability to create was a gift. In
such a world flourished invulnerable assurance and natural
humility.[1]

Bergman wrote this in the introduction to the script of *The Seventh Seal*.
The interest lies not only in the statement itself but also in his decision
to place it as a signpost to what is his most widely known and arguably
most influential film. Is he claiming something for the film, is he
reclaiming his own past or is he declaring a truth which he wishes to be
universally acknowledged?

For there is a catch, in the paragraph which immediately follows:

Today the individual has become the highest form and the
greatest bane of artistic creation. The smallest wound or pain of
the ego is examined under a microscope as if it were of eternal
importance. The artist considers his isolation, his subjectivity, his
individualism almost holy. Thus we finally gather in one large
pen, where we stand and bleat about our loneliness without
listening to each other and without realising that we are
smothering each other to death. The individualists stare into each
other's eyes and yet deny the existence of each other. We walk in
circles, so limited by our own anxieties that we can no longer
distinguish between true and false.[2]

Just as the opening paragraph can be seen to apply to *The Seventh Seal* and other films Bergman made in the 50s, so the second paragraph could be said to apply to *Persona* and *Scenes from a Marriage* and other films he made in the 60s and 70s. Like many other great artists, Bergman can face both ways. As some of his films redefined the force of religious art, the power of the sacramental, the resonance of a moral-aesthetic imperative, so others appear to cast out all of that and, with no less skill and with no less art, stand for the bleak and alienated individual of twentieth-century modernism.

Yet the undertow of religious essentiality in art persists in his introductory remarks. Having described the legend of Chartres – burnt down and reconstructed by thousands of builders and craftsmen, none with a name, so that 'no one knows to this day who built the Cathedral of Chartres[3] – he concludes with what reads like a profound credo:

> Thus if I am asked what I would like the general purpose of my films to be, I would reply that I want to be one of the artists in the cathedral on the great plain. I want to make a dragon's head, an angel, a devil – or perhaps a saint – out of stone. It does not matter which; it is the sense of satisfaction that counts. Regardless of whether I believe or not, whether I am a Christian or not, I would play my part in the collective building of the cathedral.[4]

There is more than a suggestion there that art is religion whether we believe or not. That in the end it will last only as long as it aspires to or fits into some collective cathedral which alone is the lasting temple of art. It is noteworthy that Bergman wants to make something out of 'stone'. Obviously a metaphor, but just as obviously he wants to be associated with what appears to be the most lasting of materials – forgetting, for the moment, Ozymandias. The cathedral can be seen as the sum of all the great art – all art, in Bergman's view – strained through a religious vision or even an unconscious intention. It can also be seen as the collective endeavour which film-making is and which is so much a part of his enjoyment and commitment to it. And the cathedral, where congregations gather to see the great illuminated stories in glass, to watch the ritual performances on the stage of the altar, to follow, through the calendar, the great epic of Christianity with its heroes, its villains, its disputes and digressions, its strange character parts, its compelling story-line, can be seen as the cinema of the pre-celluloid era.

Even though he himself has contributed vividly to the cinema of alienation, the cinema of the dispossessed individual, the post-Christian, fallen world of the second half of this century, we must take his seriousness about the connection between art and religion for what it is: the governing test of a film-maker whose intelligence and curiosity have inspired some of the finest films ever made. Bergman, in my opinion, is one of the dozen or so master film-makers of the century; and one of the marks of his genius, when he is at his best, is the intensity of what can only be called a vision of life. This can be almost unbearably bleak, though redeemed by stoicism in *Winter Light*; eroticism in *Summer with Monika*; womanism and tenderness in *Cries and Whispers*; or religion, in a line which takes him back to his beloved Chartres, in *The Seventh Seal*. His thesis would be challenged by many who would produce pagan, heathen, secular, atheistic, even irreligious artists, and whole centuries of artistic achievement which only by the loosest connection could be said to qualify and pass the Bergman test. Yet for him it was, and is, a profound and informing truth. And if ever it needed an exemplar, *The Seventh Seal* is first in line.

Bergman's statement here reminds me of a *cri de coeur* I once heard from a Welsh painter and poet-novelist, David Jones. He was being interviewed on television – a unique appearance which took us into the one-roomed studio-bedroom he lived in at Harrow on the Hill, a suburb on the northern rim of London. He was a Catholic; according to T. S. Eliot among others, an artist of greatness – and an innocent whose life was largely confined to this one amazingly cluttered room in a small hotel. The interview concerned his views, explained with great circumspection in the essay 'Art and Sacrament'.[5] Pushed on the critical point, that of the essential, as he saw it, link between man the maker and man the moral being, he cried out, 'If there isn't a connection, then it's all *balls*!' By then he had utterly forgotten the camera: it was the cry of someone on the razor-edge of doubt and perhaps even shouting in that dark to reassure or to recharge himself. Whatever it was, it had to be claimed. Bergman too from what, superficially, could seem a religious background greatly different from David Jones's Catholicism feels impelled to claim it. 'It is my opinion that art lost its basic creative drive the moment it was separated from worship.'[6] We must take him at his word and see *The Seventh Seal* from the outset as Bergman's attempt to keep that link: the link between creation and worship and the link between the mid-twentieth century, the Middle Ages, the New Testament and much deeper into the past.

Yet even when we look at the artefacts from ancient Mexico, Egypt, Assyria or Aboriginal Australia and so many antique civilisations, let alone the variety of work left by the Greeks, we are struck both by the religious and the secular nature of the works. Those clearly designed to fit in with the governing theology, bow to the belief of the tribe, conform to worship, and those made by 'man/woman the maker' for the sake of the thing itself, for the hell of it as opposed to the Heaven of it. Even in Chartres there are carvings which show the carver showing his own skill, taking a little of the glory to himself as well as offering so much to his God. Even in that which is ostensibly devoted to the imperative of worship, there is always space made by the individual, the artist, the mischief-maker perhaps, the side of Bergman which gives him the skills to *be* the worshipper through cinema and in cinema that he aimed to be.

Of course, many questions are begged even in one of his apparently simple sentences – what is a 'basic creative drive'? When and how was it separated from worship and what was the more precise quality of the worship? Nor is art itself a small and easily understood, casually accepted factor in this question. But we can go along with the idea without, I think, misrepresenting or misunderstanding it. Moreover, in *The Seventh Seal* itself, Bergman gives us directions and instances throughout.

Lindsay Anderson, the British film director who did the commentary for Thames Television's two-hour study of Bergman, said that in *The Seventh Seal*, 'Bergman influenced a whole generation of film-makers and film-goers.'[7] I would suggest that this influence spreads now beyond the one generation. As television recycles old movies and art-houses reach out for cheap and cult re-runs, the Bergman oeuvre grows in importance both as an example of what one man could achieve on what were very often small, even meagre, resources and as a number of films which take on territory few dare enter with any confidence. There is a Bergman world. It is a landscape lit by the finely modulated greys of Northern European light; it has intensity and intelligence in equal measure; it can be charming and comic and erotic and playful, but this is a place where the shadow is as important as the living figure and the inwardness of life is as demanding as anything that happens in the world outside. It is a cultivated world, a thinking world, above all perhaps a world trying to answer the questions which cannot be answered. For many, the clearest statement of all Bergman's preoccupations is expressed with the simplicity of genius in *The Seventh Seal*.

2

. . . .

ON FIRST MEETING INGMAR BERGMAN

It can seem a long way from Wigton and 'the pictures' in the 1940s to Oxford and Bergman at the end of the 50s. The small Cumbrian town in which I grew up was in much closer touch with the age of the gas-lit theatre than with the century of the moving image. In fact, small as it was, it welcomed a repertory company each year which came for a few months, lodged in the town and put on plays in the upstairs room of the Parish Rooms, Mondays to Saturdays.

The cinema was called 'The Palace' and I first became aware of it during the last year or two of the war. I was born in 1939, and like millions of others I grew up with the cinema. It was the one exotic plant in a dour, soberly dressed, religious and some might say rather drab town, as so many were in Britain during and after the war. The cinema was a wonder. It brought us people and stories we did not quite dare to believe were true or in any way part of the *real* business of life, which was the factory, the pub, the washing on a wet day, the grim emptiness of Sunday, the repressed words flaring up into Saturday-night brawls. We were overwhelmed but also, I think, generally outside the experience – it is possible to suffer those two conditions in harness! The cowboy films with the fake bullets, the fixed fights, the splendour of the simple morality tale, were as fantastical as Sabu or the Wizard of Oz or Tarzan and even the World War II sagas. In those we were supposed to recognise our fathers and our brothers, but I remember few moments when those who had been through it gave an indication of real recognition.

All films, the flicks, the pictures, were Another World, best of all captured in musicals where people lived in an impossible way – singing and dancing all the time – or gangster movies where equally unbeliev-able people talked with guns and broke all speed limits in their wonderful cars, or comedies perhaps most welcome of all, the Three Stooges, Abbott and Costello, Jerry Lewis, the triumphs of Ealing, hundreds of men and a few women who knew how to make you laugh. Superficial tricks and habits were appropriated, a phrase, the handling of a cigarette, the set of a hat, but there was little notion that this was the authentic portrait of a shared territory, a common experience.

In Britain, particularly in the 60s and 70s, television was to perform that social documentary function in a remarkably comprehensive way. True, some films were watched by millions of people, and sometimes – *The Grapes of Wrath* would be an instance – they would be told the story of their lives: mostly, though, they watched others, the tailored lives of Hollywood, the bespoke suiting of the British studios and never, in Wigton, a foreign, i.e. non-English speaking, film in sight. It was a world which strayed into our own real world only rarely and briefly: it was all the more enjoyed perhaps for its distance, for the news it brought of those fabulous places, amazing costumes, inaccessible bedrooms and suites and kitchens, and wild adventurers tamed to a happy ending with eternal and faithful and most likely virgin love the only way it happened.

Yet what did it matter? Like so many others, I was happily obsessed with the movies. For many years I went two or more often three times a week, thus catching all three films – Mr Cusack, owner of The Palace, ran a brisk repertory system with new films on Mondays, Wednesdays and Fridays, each running for two days, and a Saturday Matinee which, if the Friday films were suitable, contained a chance to see the end of the week show. I had favourite seats which developed as gangs grew and fell away, as girlfriends came and became more demanding. It was a rowdy place sometimes – *Cinema Paradiso* captured a lot of it – and for many years in the 40s and 50s it was as packed as the Tuesday cattle auction or the Saturday night pub with its own characters and threads of contact. To miss a good picture was to feel deprived and envious of those who had seen it and would be nagged to reveal the secret of its power. No doubt the careful surface morality as well as the occasional innuendo and subversive body language sank through my gaping consciousness every bit as forcefully as the direct images transfixed my attention. To extricate the influence of the cinema on anyone who went as often as I did – and there were millions of us – would take a longer book than this, and this must return to Bergman.

He, at the end of the 1950s, I believe single-handedly in my case, spliced together the life I was leading and the life in a film. *The Seventh Seal* was a very big factor in this, but an even bigger initiating factor was *Summer with Monika*. And here, the distance between Wigton and Bergman was not so very great.

Harriet Andersson in *Summer With Monika*

Summer with Monika spoke to the condition of many adolescents in the 50s: it could have been my story or that of thousands of others. The nerve of it was that somehow and for the first time, I think, a film tapped itself into the real root of what I knew I had in some measure or would in some measure or wanted in some measure to experience. The bait was Harriet Andersson.

She was a new type of woman. We had seen Rita Hayworth and Ava Gardner, Elizabeth Taylor and Jane Russell, the English beauties and the Mid-Western corkers. But although there were now and then certain correspondences, they were not so much brought to us on the screen as separated from us by the screen, tantalisingly behind the celluloid, creatures in a fabulous aquarium. Such sex as there was lay mainly in the land of the obvious bosoms, the twirled skirt showing the knickers or the languorous embrace. There was a top-spin in some films for those who knew, who had been there, who could pick up the clues, but it was rare for beginners to feel much more than a disturbing excitement and now and then a disappointed puzzlement.

Harriet Andersson blew that away. She was eighteen or nineteen and looked the eighteen or nineteen of a modern late-50s girl – not the strapped and laced eighteen or nineteen of the virgin woman in embryo we were all used to on the Big Screen. Harriet Andersson could have stepped out of the screen and into the streets of Wigton any day. She would have attracted a lot of (then) polite vulgar attention, but she would not have been too far ahead of the erotic teasing to be seen in buttoned cardigans and complicit smiles in and around a town where slowly the ice of publicly policed and often privately suppressed sex was beginning to break. Harriet Andersson could have been the sexy girl at the school any number of us went to. It was she who drew me in – from photographs modestly displayed outside the Scala Cinema in Walton Street in Oxford. Once in, her mores and her attitudes struck chord on chord and *here*, in what was the first homesick term at a university whose codes were often haughty and tedious, speaking in a foreign tongue which we thought it a good joke to describe as English dragged backwards, was a film which made a direct impact on all the senses that cried out to be recognised as being of their time.

Harriet Andersson's erotic charm, her playfulness and sense of life – subsumed in her great acting talent – struck with the shock of recognition. The last sequence made me hate her and lust after her in equal and unbearable conflict.

Though it was mostly the performance of Harriet Andersson which called me into Bergman's world, there was more. The landscape, for instance, was not unlike the northern landscape I knew, the quality of the light, the sense of space and the possibility of solitude, the vast, grey sky, the occasional release of a short summer. More than that, though, was a seriousness of intention which I absorbed, registered in some shelf of the brain, but did not take out to examine until much later. Bergman has a deep seriousness about intense emotional relationships which I find sympathetic and with which I find it easy to identify. More than that, I consider it to be the most honest and truthful way to take on life – despite the proximity of seriousness to earnestness, pomposity and boringness and even despite the unease many feel with the fullest weight of expression of an emotion. In Bergman, people are mostly very serious about what he thinks to be serious matters: Love, Death, Religion, Art. Indeed it is his resolute preoccupation with serious concerns – even in his few comedies – that mark him out and perhaps account for his having rather fallen out of fashion recently. The seriousness and the insistence on taking on the whole of life, not a slice or a bite, the circumference of existence and what is above it, has been his chief matter, and this, together with the religious pulse, makes him somewhat alien to a post-modern and largely disbelieving world.

Perhaps there was a religious tone even in *Summer with Monika* – a paganism for sure, underscored, as one learned later, by Bergman's own affair with Harriet Andersson. (Knowing that, it is now impossible to see the film without regarding it as in some way a love poem to her.) Certainly in *The Seventh Seal* the religious nature of Bergman's work came through immediately and was the binding thread of the film.

Schooled by Monika, I willingly submitted to *The Seventh Seal* and found it, if anything, an even more direct penetration. *Summer with Monika* had brought to the screen the spectrum of possibilities in adolescent love and lust: its wildness, its idealism, its desperate searching for the centre of existence, its jealousy and abrupt cruelties. It was a portrait of the present that I saw and to some extent lived in. And it was, at the most primitive level, 'sexy' in a direct, unHollywood, uncoded way. Perhaps the foreignness of the speech gave it an extra twist or perhaps that strange tongue enabled the message or the truth of the story to go in more directly, more deeply, just as comedy can sometimes 'deliver' ideas much more effectively than a sober or earnest drama. And Bergman's own real passion for Harriet Andersson must also have been a factor: he was well into his stride by then as a film-maker and increasingly able to put on to celluloid the deepest feelings he held. In *The Seventh Seal* those feelings were about Death and God and, to a lesser but integral extent, art and love. God and Death, though, were the great pillars, and it was here that he completely captured my attention and commanded an admiration, even a love, for his work which has not slackened.

For he used what had been 'just the pictures', 'the common old flick' at the Palace, Wigton, sometimes as much a place for hanging out as for seeing the film, to portray and explore what seemed to me then the very deepest matters of existence. It was as if Albert Camus had begun to appear in the *Wizard* next to Wilson. The medium which, however enrapturing, had been taken as a convenience, like a tap; the medium which, in my experience of it in that town, had conveyed religious ideas, for instance, only in the retrospectively intriguing but at the time ponderous and (privately, guiltily) unbelievable bible-conforming Hollywood Testamental-Epics. Sometimes a good novel had been dramatised for the screen, and undoubtedly the hidden agendas of the hard 'tec stories were given unfair short shrift, but generally the screen was for entertainment: for the real stuff of thought you opened a book. Bergman upended all that in the one film.

And it was the opening of a door. From Bergman I and a generation sought out De Sica, Fellini, Visconti, Rossellini, Carné, Renoir, Truffaut, Buñuel, Kurosawa, Ray – on and on they stretch, the squadrons of 'foreign' film-makers telling stories from an adult literary point of view, informed with all the arts of the best novelists, absorbed in the tradition of high thinking and ambition, but welded to this medium which, despite its capacity to breed geniuses and colonise a whole culture, had still seemed to the majority of its fans obstinately out of the race when weighty concerns were to be addressed. Later, older, more experienced in looking at films, I would realise that some of what I had seen as a boy and let float as mere entertainment had sent down lines which could draw up some of the same recognition so clearly expressed by Bergman. But that was later. At the time, 1958, when I was nineteen, *The Seventh Seal* came with the force of *Sons and Lovers* or *L'Etranger*, *Portrait of the Artist as a Young Man*, *Under Milk Wood* or *Buddenbrooks*. By some curious alchemy, it seemed not only to speak to my condition with a precision that was almost hallucinatory, it said what I would have said could I have articulated and organised it by myself.

This is well known to everyone, everyone who allows himself/herself to be open to and so touched by a work whether it is a Beatles number, a Merce Cunningham ballet, a Rembrandt self-portrait, a poem by Hardy, a television play by Alan Bennett (or later by Bergman himself). There is the whispered, rather worrying but unmistakable feeling that this is specifically for and about you – even if it by no means fits into your life with all neatness. In a vague but nonetheless palpable sense, the thing sings your song.

You have to be ready for it. I was ready for *The Seventh Seal*. Just as I was unprepared to be jolted and absorbed in what could almost be described as a literary way by 'the pictures' in Wigton, so I was all too prepared for the subject and content of this later film at university. Bergman leapt across the barrier which had separated the movie experience from the literary or 'arts' experience through the power and the telling of his story. For this undoubtedly was a film to which ideas were as important as in any novel or play. I had read Ibsen and Strindberg and seen one or two performances of plays by those and other major masters on BBC television – a special Sunday-night date in the house of an uncle. *The Seventh Seal* breathed that air and from then on, instantly, the pictures became the movies, even became 'cinema' and 'film' for a few pretentious months and then sank back to the movies, but never to the mere passing flicks and indifferently appreciated flickerings of a blissfully hieratic childhood which had accepted the propaganda of schooled snobbish grading rather than the immediate and telling evidence of excited senses, addiction and absorption in the material. In short, Bergman – others too, but Bergman most of all – put films on my Arts map and inspired the immediate ambition to become a film critic on the university newspaper, make a film myself and thereafter be near and around films ever since. But that is to jump ahead.

You have to be ready for a conversion. Clearly there was some inkling in me that the mass of celluloid I had seen and served between the ages of about five and eighteen had been more significant than my old-fashioned cultural education would allow. More important, though, was the subject of *The Seventh Seal*.

The story is simple enough. A Knight and his Squire return from the Crusades. Their country is ravaged by the plague. They meet Death and the Knight makes a bargain: as long as he can hold him off in a game of chess, his life will be spared. As they journey through their native country they encounter artists, fanatics, thieves, mere rogues, but everywhere the presence of Death, who proceeds to win the game by fair means and foul. At the end, all but the artists are gathered up by him. Intellectually the film is bound together by the two strands of the Knight's desperate search for some proof, some confirmation of his faith, and the Squire's view that there is nothing beyond the present flesh but emptiness.

At that time I was still a practising Christian. I had been in the choir since the age of six, after that a server, a regular communicant. The church's place in my life, in the life of many in that time and in such communities, was not only strong, it was implacable. Going away to university, at a time when it was not uncommon to see the college chapel well filled on a Sunday, had coincided with a climactic turbulence in beliefs which had been questioned only unconsciously and in public handled with apprehensive respect. *The Seventh Seal*, on a medium which had the power of finding me totally unprepared for it, articulated the questions I realised that I had not dared ask myself. What were the realistically true signs that a God existed? Where was the consistent evidence of any divine benevolence? What was the point of prayer? Was the idea of a personal, involved God entirely vain? The passion of the Knight's doubts exploded my own, his determination to hold on to the outward exercises of belief when the inward credo had crumbled coincided precisely with my own situation. We are never as ready to be convinced as when we are secretly of the same persuasion in the first place and *The Seventh Seal* swept me into its simple perhaps but compelling and utterly modern view of the relationship between God and Man. I listened to the Squire's agnostic subversion but at that time I was still too dipped in the church to admit any force in it. In the agony of the Knight I saw enlarged, and made as unequivocal as a stained glass window, my own distress.

It was at that time too that I was discovering the Dark Ages in English History. Somehow at school we had skipped through it very lightly: the Romans to Alfred the Great with not a lot in between. There was not a lot in between in terms of scholarship fit for a schoolboy. At university, however, an enthusiastic tutor made this for me the most vivid part of the whole three-year experience of reading History. It was a time of heroic scholarship, brutal warlords and desperately necessary devotion. It is a time which has intrigued me ever since, but in 1958 it was a revelation. Again, analyses of one's own condition are embarrassing but probably germane. As important was the fact that a significant part of this history happened on or near my turf. The men and women flowed in from Ireland through Cumbria – where I had been brought up – across the remains of the Roman Wall – which I had already walked several times – towards Jarrow or Lindisfarne. Or they came down from the West of Scotland, perhaps from Iona – which had been the site of a memorable Christian holiday – and down through the northern landscapes to the same north-eastern sanctuaries. Foolishly no doubt, I felt a direct kinship.

Bergman's film is set at least six hundred years on from the centre of my academic interest at university. But there's a great deal in common: from the over-arching importance of religion, to the food, the weapons, the sense of a time dedicated to a divine presence and an eternal mystery. More of a seamless mood probably; rather bad history, I suspect, nearer to a dream of a time than the reality of it. And in Bergman's physical landscapes I saw yet another connection. Although both the history and the landscape were by no means the same, there were enough similarities to give me a feeling of personal possession.

The film's strengths as story-telling, as characterisation, as argument and medieval counterfeit, will be considered later. In this autobiographical section, it is enough to say that I was converted.

I became the film critic of *Cherwell*, the university newspaper; made a film with Gavin Millar, and others; went into the BBC, where I was working with film within a year or two; moved on to write television films on Debussy and Douanier Rousseau for Ken Russell; and then wrote a few feature films, preferring in the end to pull out of that world and stay in the area of Arts films, where it seemed to me an editor and writer – which is what I am – could make a more substantial contribution and work in a documentary or docu-drama form which was as interesting and certainly more fertile than most of what was going on in the British Film Industry at that time or since.

In that capacity, years on, I started an arts programme, 'The South Bank Show', and the first week or so wrote to Bergman to request an interview around which we could build a film. At that time, 1978, he was in Germany, having dismissed Sweden for humiliating him, as he saw it, over taxes.

I think that this was the first time he had agreed to an extensive interview on British television and his behaviour was intriguing. First he asked me to go to Munich for what in effect became an interview: he interviewing me. We met in a small set of rooms in the studio; his wife prepared the strange souplike slop he always had for lunch – I remember what he ate, not what we ate. Quite simply he turned the tables and in effect asked me about his movies. It was a cross-examination I was relieved and delighted to undergo. Relieved because I had wondered what I could possibly say to this man who, over the years, had become a lodestar. Delighted because it was one examination for which I was totally primed.

We agreed to do the filming a fortnight or so later in the Munich studios. They would provide us with a small room. After we had set up the camera and the lights and the microphones, Bergman arrived and in the most genial way redisposed the set and the equipment. He was particularly keen to have the door behind his chair open and also persuaded us to bring the two hard chairs much closer together. Before the interview began he let out a fart-like snort and beamed.

Some of what he said is more relevant to other parts of this book and some of it he had said before, as I now discover, and has said with some slight variations mostly consonant with a carelessness about detail ever since. Nevertheless, it was my first encounter and to me each sentence was a Revelation.

Cinema, he began, was 'to me an obsession'.[8] He said, 'I saw my first picture when I was six years old and I was completely lost.' He wanted 'most of all' to have a projector of his own. Come Christmas, there was the unmistakable outline of a projector all wrapped up but addressed to his brother. Bergman promptly 'bought' it from him with his collection of lead soldiers. He gave him 'the whole army', he told me; on other occasions he has said he gave him half his army. The career was begun.

Like so many who achieve greatness in the arts – as in crafts, sciences, athletics, the circus, I suppose – passionate and dedicated early beginnings seem all but a *sine qua non*. There are, there always are, exceptions. But Bergman ran true to form. In his beginning was his end. There is much more in that childhood which contributed to the personality and culture and romantic obsession of Bergman, but his declared instant 'obsession' with the cinema is centrally important. Happy the man or woman whose obsession can turn into a life's work. And if – as I guess he did – he meant the word in its strictest sense, then we can understand the overflowing into forty films made by the time he was seventy, besides innumerable screenplays, radio plays, stage plays, stage and radio and opera productions – all feeding into the obsession with the cinema as did the richness and variety of that severe, tormented, critically aware, imaginative childhood.

Summer Interlude was another of his films I saw in that first year at university, and he said 'It is close to my heart. For the first time

Ingmar Bergman with Inga Landgré

something worked.'[9] It was 'very personal', he said, it had 'to do with me very much'. Love, he more than implied, had come right: his own emotional life, which has been such a moving parallel to his films, often the quarry for the subjects, always the engine for the themes, was firing on all the cylinders he wanted. 'Some pictures grow old beautifully,' he said, implying that *Summer Interlude* was one such. 'Others just grow old and it would be better if they just disappeared like theatre productions.'

A restatement of the intense relationship he has with his films came when discussing *Sawdust and Tinsel*. We showed the clip of that terrible sequence where Frost the clown goes down to the beach to rescue his foolish naked wife from the manhandling and jeers of the soldiers and then has to carry her back over jagged stones to the circus tent. 'I am a very jealous man,' said Bergman. 'I tried to find a solution in this very brutal film.'[10] Throughout the interview he maintained that he used his films to face up to his personal fears. 'I am afraid of most things in this world that exist,' he said.

In *The Seventh Seal* he was facing up to his fear of Death. 'Death is present the whole time in this picture and everybody in this picture reacts differently to Death. After that picture I still think about Death but it is not an obsession any more.'[11] The making of the movie as a therapy? Or does the picture coincide with a phase in Bergman's life through which he would have travelled without making the movie?

Death appears as a monk, I said. 'Or a clown,' Bergman replied.

The ambiguity could not be more succinctly stated. I went for the religious jugular, which is where the film affected me; more than twenty years on from the making of it, Bergman introduced me to an interpretation which seems less convincing as the film goes on but is certainly a strain which the character Death can bear. If he is 'like' a monk, then he is the devil's monk, but monklike he dresses and indeed later in the film he impersonates a monk to gain an advantage over the Knight. If he is a clown, with all the wisdom and weary overview of life that a Bergman clown would bring to bear, then he is like Lear's Fool and playing a most serious role, clown as true voice of reality, not clown as comic.

'He is a man,' I said, 'not a presence.'

'Yes,' Bergman agreed. 'That is the fascination of the stage or the cinema. If you take a chair, a perfectly normal chair, and say "This is the most expensive and fantastic wonderful chair made in the whole world" – if you say that, everybody will believe it. If the Knight says, "You are Death", you believe it.'[12]

Throughout the interview he was helpful and, I thought, as honest as he could be. His figure is a huddle of limbs; his face long, hair lank, face white – he hates the sun – eyes deep and mesmeric, seriousness not in doubt and yet now and then a hoot of laughter. After a while he requested a rest and we went next door where he lay on a camp bed and recomposed himself. He has been ill – stomach ulcers real and imagined since he was young – and some of his best work has been done in convalescence. At the end of the interview he rushed over to hug and embrace me, which was unexpected. I had thought him thoroughly distanced, not having read and learnt at that time how emotional and passionate he could be and was so often with those who worked with him. There's a madcap, ebullient side of Bergman which the overall portrait sometimes misses. 'Even in the most tragic scenes,' he said in that interview, 'there must be some joy, some lust; if not, the picture is boring.'

He took a very keen interest in our film and waived his fee – he was not a rich man – so that we could afford to get the pristine negatives from the Swedish bank in which they were deposited and make the best possible transfers. My chief regret is that I did not make it a double, a two-hour programme. As it was, we snatched some extra minutes from the network but there was enough for much more.

He had indicated that he would like to keep in touch but, rightly or wrongly, I thought he was being merely polite and never wrote beyond the usual thanks. This, I suppose, is a long-delayed letter.

A couple of years ago the European Film event came to Glasgow. I was asked to do the introductions to this wide variety of films and agreed principally because Bergman was due to turn up and receive a lifetime achievement accolade. He was one of the panel of judges for the best films in different categories but he never made the Award Ceremony. The stomach, we were told, had once more laid him low. Stuck on the platform, I thought it served me right for expecting a magician to appear for however material a prize. The stomach was possibly telling him that another script was coming on and, rightly, he went along with that.

3

....
THE PLAY'S THE THING

I was teaching at the Theatre School in Malmö [this was in 1955]. There were some youngsters there, eight or nine of them, and I was looking for a play to put on for that's the best way of teaching. I couldn't find anything, so I took it into my head to write something myself. It was called *A Painting on Wood*.

It is a pure training play and consists of a number of monologues. All except for one part. One pupil was being trained for the musical comedy section. He had a good singing voice and looked very handsome, but as soon as he opened his mouth it was a catastrophe. So I gave him a silent part. The Saracens had cut his tongue out. He was the Knight. I worked it up with my pupils and put it on.

Then, if I remember aright, it suddenly struck me one day I ought to make a film of the play: so I started on the script. The whole thing developed quite naturally. My stomach had been in bad shape and I sat writing this film in Karolinska Hospital in Stockholm while it was being put to rights. I handed the script to S.F. (Svensk Filmindustri) and S.F. said 'No thank you'. But then came the success of *Smiles of a Summer Night* and I got permission to make it, providing I did it in thirty-five days. So I shot in thirty-five days and it was ever so cheap and ever so simple.[13]

In Peter Cowie's critical biography of Bergman,[14] the origin of *The Seventh Seal* is made to seem a little less simple. With typical thoroughness, he explores the film's route from stage to screen, giving us more elaboration than Bergman suggests. It is often Bergman's way – in an interview – to concentrate on the puff of deceptively simple magic which flashes the film into life. Perhaps he is not too vain to give much serious attention to what is past, and so the quicker it can be disposed of the better. Or maybe he really does remember as simple what on examination seems less so to others.

The original one-act play for ten students (who included Gunnar Björnstrand) in March 1955 was by Bergman himself. But according to

Cowie, 'The performance that took the critics by storm however was on September 16th of the same year when a different cast (this time including Bibi Andersson) played "Wood Painting" [as Cowie translates it] at the Royal Dramatic Theatre in Stockholm under the direction of Bengt Ekerot, a member of the 40-talisterna, an accomplished stage director and the man who would play Death in *The Seventh Seal*.'

Cowie then points out elements in *A Painting on Wood* which found their way into the final film script: the fear of the plague, the burning of the witch, the Dance of Death. However, there is no chess game between Death and the Knight (who is without speech, as noted, in the play; in continuous dialogue with God in the film), nor are the artistic clowning 'holy couple' of Jof and Mia – Joseph and Mary with their infant – there. The smith and his strumpet wife are there but, Cowie concludes, 'Only one character may be found full-blown, and that is Jons the Squire, whose dialogue in play and film is almost identical line for line.'[15] Gunnar Björnstrand, who played the part in Bergman's original production, transferred it to the screen.

The deeper preoccupations of the film can be traced back to Bergman's childhood in an intense – for him suffocatingly, oppressively tense – Christian home where the great questions of the relationship between Good and Evil, God and the Devil, Man and God, Man and Death and Redemption were part of daily life and conversation. His father, a pastor in the Lutheran Church, addicted to all its high rituals and strict forms, was the tyrannical domestic Godhead. Although he rebelled against his family and his background, his introduction to *The Seventh Seal* shows how close he kept to it in essentials. 'He often,' writes Cowie, 'signs his scripts with the initials S.D.G. (Soli Deo Gloria – To God Alone the Glory) as J. S. Bach did at the end of every composition.'[16]

In the 1950s, when Bergman was in his late thirties, the religious significance of Death informed at least three films: *The Seventh Seal*, *Wild Strawberries* and *The Magician* (also known as *The Face*).

In 1955, he was still influenced by medieval frescoes he had seen as murals in Swedish churches. At the beginning of the play *A Painting on Wood*, Bergman states that his story is taken directly from a fresco in a church in southern Sweden. Bergman's cultural well was deep and his taproot to Scandinavian culture profound. Swedenborg and Kirkegaard as much as Sibelius and Swedish history influenced him. But most of all in his own language there was Strindberg. There were also those whose influence could be directly felt, such as the playwright Hjalmar Bergman.

The theatre and the opera invade many of Bergman's films in content, style, casting and tone. Any other artist would be content with the life Bergman has enjoyed as a director and author for the stage. He has written some twenty-three plays, none of which is in the classic repertory but one of which, *The Death of Punch*, was so successful that it set him off on a career as a scriptwriter. As importantly, he was a theatre director. He began directing amateurs and small groups in his late teens and continued throughout his career to direct at least two, sometimes more, plays, beside the occasional opera, the inevitable radio play (often scripted by himself) and the film and sometimes two films. His output is that of the monumental nineteenth-century craftsman/ artist.

So by the time he came to write *A Painting on Wood* he had directed plays by Shakespeare, Strindberg, Camus, Chesterton, Anouilh, Tennessee Williams, Pirandello, Lehar, Molière, Ostrovsky – and many by Ingmar Bergman. Habits of work, profound friendships, ways of seeing how words and actions could be dramatised not only for the stage but for effective transfer to the screen were practised in these productions. Bergman is widely known for his cinematic grasp, his technical understanding of camera, lights, the editing process, the character and qualities of celluloid and sound. He is also a man of immense theatrical achievements which some think are antipathetical to film. Bergman is one of the few directors who crosses the line between stage and screen; indeed, in his work it seems that the one feeds the other. The usual polar categorisations are irrelevant to his work – that theatre actors are too externalised, too big, altogether too loud to work on the inward, intimate yet giant projecting camera; that the play exists in a live 'time' which is of no use to the camera; that words are the leading players in one medium and mainly a supporting cast in the other; that certain subjects are theatrical and can never be anything else, and so on. Bergman just ignores all this, and nowhere can it be more plainly seen than in *The Seventh Seal*, which swept his name around the world as a picture but which as a screenplay reads like and could, but for a few touches, be mounted as a stage play.

Indeed, in the published version he sets it out like a stage play. Here we have no 'Long shot', 'Close-up', 'Zoom' or 'Pan'; no EXTERIOR DAY FOREST; no INTERIOR NIGHT TAVERN: there is the austerity of a stage play and a stage play with comparatively few directions. The action is in the words which tell the story and the words of the story tell the action. It was of course numbered – shot by shot – in the shooting script, but Bergman has deliberately chosen to delete that in the published version *and it doesn't much matter.*

Before quoting to emphasise this point, I would like to point out yet another influence on Bergman which is rarely given its full weight. Radio. Bergman wrote prolifically for Swedish radio and the medium fascinated him as much as it fascinated the young Orson Welles. The three primary elements in radio are: the utter reliance on words and sounds; the necessity for strictly linear story-telling; the collusion with the imagination of the listener. All those qualities are found in many a Bergman film and *The Seventh Seal* is one of the finest examples. Just as it could transfer back to the stage from which it sprang without much effort, so, even more effortlessly, could it be given as a radio play. Indeed, I have tried the experiment of closing my eyes and merely

Bergman lining up a shot

listening to the film (admittedly from the privileged position of someone who knows it well) and the effect is still powerful.

It is Bergman's theatrical insistence on the clarity of dialogue, and the influence of sound and sound effects – both honed in radio – which gives it such immediacy. As for the story-telling, he is a master of the basic narrative, seamlessly using plot developments such as cliff-hangers, questions which demand answers, mines laid which we know will explode later, and all the trickery or craftedness of the narrative form. But it is his reliance on the audience's imagination that shows his affinity with radio and perhaps its influence on him. Just as *The Seventh Seal*, though set six or seven hundred years after the Early Dark Ages which were my study at university, could draw me in because it touched imaginatively on a whole former world which belonged with witches and horses, starvation, plagues and faith, so within the film he relies on our imaginations again and again.

A great and dense primeval forest is suggested by a few trees. A whole country in torment and the insanity of fanaticism is conveyed by the arrival of a small crowd of flagellants in a village; the visions of a pure man are etched in with a literalness which beckons us to miracles and worlds above or parallel to our own. Bergman seems to know how the particular can not only represent the general but stir us to weave our own stories in support of his. When the Squire, for instance, discovers the dumb girl in the looted, otherwise empty village and then comes across the man who sent his master to the Crusades and is now a thief and potential rapist, we 'see' the razing of the village, we 'understand' her dumbness (now explained), we 'sense' the deformation of a society in which a theological Doctor can be reduced to a thuggish criminal. Or to take what might seem a very strained example: when the Knight and his Squire are riding on horseback together for the very few film moments allotted that sequence, am I alone in sensing the drudgery of great wasted treks across Europe and into the Holy Land, the sun merciless, the road lonely, the objective in dispute? Death, whether as the monk or the 'clown', is another more obvious call on our imaginations, but in the few scenes he has we are moved by Bergman's skill and the actor's response to know him as diabolic, playful, deceitful, though honest in his way, capable of comedy (sawing down the tree), in the end implacable.

The screenplay opens very like a play:

The night had brought little relief from the heat, and at dawn a hot gust of wind blows across the colourless sea. The KNIGHT, Antonius Block, lies prostrate on some spruce branches spread upon the fine sand. His eyes are wide open and bloodshot from lack of sleep.

Nearby his SQUIRE, Jons, is snoring loudly. He has fallen asleep where he collapsed, at the edge of the forest among the wind-gnarled fir trees. His open mouth gapes towards the dawn and unearthly sounds come from his throat.

At the sudden gust of wind the horses stir, stretching their parched muzzles towards the sea. They are as thin and worn as their masters.[17]

'A great and dense primeval forest is suggested by a few trees.'

The horses are the first indication of what might not be available for the stage, but they are scarcely essential and the presence of horses, off-stage, could easily be established. The script goes on:

> The KNIGHT has risen and waded into the shallow water, where he rinses his sunburned face and blistered lips.
>
> JONS rolls over to face the forest and the darkness.[18]

There is reference to the sky and a seagull – again, very possible to 'stage' – and then the brief introduction to what Bergman calls the 'complete screenplay' ends, most theatrically. The Knight has washed and prayed. He turns round.

> Behind him stands a man in black. His face is very pale and he keeps his hands hidden in the wide folds of his cloak.
>
> KNIGHT: Who are you?
> DEATH: I am Death.
> KNIGHT: Have you come for me?
> DEATH: I have been walking by your side for a long time.
> KNIGHT: That I know.
> DEATH: Are you prepared?
> KNIGHT: My body is frightened, but I am not.
> DEATH: Well, there is no shame in that.
>
> The KNIGHT has risen to his feet. He shivers. DEATH opens his cloak to place it around the KNIGHT's shoulders.
>
> KNIGHT: Wait a moment.
> DEATH: That's what they all say. I grant no reprieves.
> KNIGHT: You play chess, don't you?
>
> A gleam of interest kindles in DEATH's eyes.
>
> DEATH: How did you know that?
> KNIGHT: I have seen it in paintings and heard it sung in ballads.
> DEATH: Yes, in fact I'm quite a good chess player.
> KNIGHT: But you can't be better than I am.

The KNIGHT rummages in the big black bag which he keeps beside him and takes out a small chessboard. He places it carefully on the ground and begins setting up the pieces.

DEATH: Why do you want to play chess with me?
KNIGHT: I have my reasons.
DEATH: That is your privilege.
KNIGHT: The condition is that I may live as long as I hold out against you. If I win, you will release me. Is it agreed?[19]

And the story is set in motion.

There is nothing there, in the rhythm or the content, which could not be done on stage. In fact you could describe the dialogue as 'stagy' even in the pejorative sense of over-formal, too literary in tone, disobeying the centrifugal force of naturalism which is such a power in film-making when it concerns characters who are set up to be believed in as human beings. But the narrative drive vaults over that criticism. Just as the actual filming – as we shall see – gives not only texture but

The game of chess

other layers to the scene. Yet the heart and purpose of the scene exist without screen, could exist without stage; they could float through the ether and still tell the same story with as much impact. By abandoning the rudimentary numbering of shots in this printed screenplay, Bergman is deliberately taking the work back to its dramatic roots and also, I think, asserting that character and dialogue are the twin stars of his universe.

If that opening scene appears too easy and pat an example, consider this, one of the most famously 'cinematic' moments in the film. It is the scene where the young girl-witch is being taken through the forest at night to be burned. The Knight, the Squire, Jof, Mia, their child, Plog the smith and his wife are travelling fearfully and with care; soldiers approach with a cart. On it is:

> The WITCH being taken to the place where she will be burned.
> Next to her eight soldiers shuffle along tiredly, carrying their
> lances on their backs. The girl sits in the cart, bound with iron
> chains around her throat and arms. She stares fixedly into the
> moonlight.
>
> A black figure sits next to her, a monk with his hood pulled
> down over his head.
>
> JONS: Where are you going?
> SOLDIER: To the place of execution.
> JONS: Yes, now I can see. It's the girl who has done it with the
> Black One. The witch?
>
> The SOLDIER nods sourly. Hesitantly, the travellers follow. The
> KNIGHT guides his horse over to the side of the cart. The WITCH
> seems to be half-conscious, but her eyes are wide open.
>
> KNIGHT: I see that they have hurt your hands.[20]

It is worth pausing to look more closely at the last two lines of dialogue. Jons is telling the audience all they need to know about this encounter without their having to see it: he is, in fact, speaking as on radio. So is the Knight. And both of them are also pushing forward the narrative. It goes on:

The WITCH's pale, childish face turns towards the KNIGHT and she shakes her head.

KNIGHT: I have a potion that will stop your pain.

She shakes her head again.

JONS: Why do you burn her at this time of night? People have so few diversions these days?
SOLDIER: Saints preserve us, be quiet! It's said she brings the Devil with her wherever she goes.
JONS: You are eight brave men, then.
SOLDIER: Well, we've been paid. And this is a volunteer job.[21]

The scene goes on to show the Knight restless to question her about the Devil so that he might move a step nearer his understanding of God, and Jons becoming more outraged at the cruelty of it and distraught at the meaningless of it all. There is nothing there which a clever director and an inventive cast could not do with a minimum of props and scenery. There is nothing that a radio audience could miss. And yet on the screen the scene flickers and glistens with all the extra atmosphere, all the tones and detail which make it vividly unforgettable. It seems to me an extraordinary strength of Bergman's that he can make a work which co-exists on these three levels and on all of them has conviction.

The way the scenes 'play' – each scene well moulded and in itself a complete statement – and the pace and poise of the dialogue give away the origin of this film. And yet it exists as a wholly successful picture. Nothing is taken away: all that is different is what is added on.

Above and overleaf: The knight and the witch

4

SEALED IN CHILDHOOD

> Sometimes I live in my childhood. When I go to sleep, just before
> going to sleep, I can go through the rooms of my grandmother –
> it can be very photographic. When I'm unhappy I fall back on
> that part of my life with my grandmother always patient and
> secure and nice.[22]

> I can still roam through the landscape of my childhood and still
> experience lights, smells, rooms. I remember nothing dull.[23]

Few childhoods have been so lavishly illustrated as Bergman's. In
Fanny and Alexander, his triumphant and masterful return to Sweden
after the tax flight to Germany, he drew on deep wells from his
upbringing. The statements quoted above show how conscious and
how serious he is about his childhood. The child was not only father to
the man: the man nursed the child in him and went back for more, often
and often.

The problem here is that Bergman's childhood is so intensely
remembered and so deeply and insistently used in his films that it is all
but impossible to indicate those aspects which most particularly affect
The Seventh Seal. Some of the main markers will, however, confirm that,
like all Bergman's best films, the themes and stories, some of the images
even, come out of a childhood which seems – as the childhoods of great
artists so often do – a perfect seedbed, however arid and difficult, for a
great flowering of talent.

Bergman was born in 1918 in Uppsala. He had a caul over his
head, long thought a sign of good fortune. His earliest times were spent
in the home of his beloved grandmother in Uppsala. His father was a
chaplain in the State Lutheran Church, and Bergman's early years were
spent in a frigid household. The Bergman family 'consisted of pastors
and farmers right back to the sixteenth century; piety, diligence and
innate conservatism were passed to each new generation.'[24] Ingmar
was the second of three children: an older brother became a diplomat, a
younger sister became a novelist.

In her book *Karin by the Sea*, Margareta Bergman wrote of her mother:

> After spending half the night indulging one of her few vices –
> reading – and having in its second half managed to scrape
> together a few hours' sleep for herself, [mother] would come
> stumbling in to breakfast only half awake and in a state of
> extreme nervous irritability, to find her freshly washed,
> matitudinally cheerful spouse, already hungry as a hunter,
> standing by the breakfast table with his gold watch in his hand.[25]

The father would begin his day

> splashing, whistling, jubilantly singing fragments of hymns....
> He would take an ice-cold shower, shave, and brush his teeth
> with the same frenzy because year in year out poor Father,
> clergyman of the State Lutheran Church as he was, lived on the
> borderline of minimum erotic subsistence.[26]

A powerful couple whose manners and tradition forbade the overt display of strong feeling between them. Bergman in his diaries notes that 'They lived completely officially, observed if you like, as a priest and his wife. Like politicians, they had no privacy.'[27] The house was full of guests: Sunday evening was the only time guarded for the sole enjoyment of the family.

Bergman's father was a powerful and charismatic preacher and his impact from the pulpit was widely noted. A photograph of him in the pulpit bears an unforgettable resemblance to another massively magnified authority figure rising in Europe throughout Bergman's adolescence. It is perhaps worth noting that his paternal grandfather, his father and his elder brother all suffered from a wasting disease which eventually paralysed or severely disabled their legs.

There was a family villa which all repaired to for the summer, but the place of his birth was the medieval town of Uppsala. It was the home of the ancient Royal Family, the Ynglings: burial mounds, a twin-towered cathedral, an antique castle nearby – for a self-confirmed daydreamer like Bergman it was a landing-pad for tales from the past.

Bergman's father in his pulpit

In *Bergman on Bergman*,[28] he describes the fourteen rooms in the
family's great apartment, each room arranged as it had been in 1890
when his grandmother had arrived there as a bride: 'lots of big rooms
with ticking clocks, enormous carpets and massive furniture ... the
combined furniture of two upper middle-class families, pictures from
Italy, palms.... I used to sit under the dining table there, "listening" to
the sunshine which came in through the cathedral windows.' It was a
house of magic and fantasy; easy to see such a child having his
imagination fed richly.

Other points from his childhood – whose backdrop was always
the piety and severity of the Lutheran church, religion impregnating
every hour of the day, and the unacknowledged tensions between a
powerful father and a passionate mother – include the six-year-old
Bergman helping the gardener take the corpses from the hospital to the
mortuary (his father had been appointed Chaplain to the Royal
Hospital, Sofia Lemmet). 'It was scary but it was also very fascinating
... for a child it was traumatic' (he watched limbs removed in surgery
being burned) 'and I loved it.'[29] There was also the Bergman
household's method of punishment. Beatings were common. Weals
were common. Humiliation was another method: when Bergman wet
his bed, which he did often as a child, he was forced to wear a red skirt
all day. 'I felt unspeakably humiliated.'[30] On the positive side there was
an old family retainer, a cook, who let him have much of his way and
seems to have given him sensual security. He needed her basic skills.
He was never far from illness, usually connected with his stomach.

His involvement with the theatre began at home – there was a
puppet playhouse he built, impressed by a visit to the Royal Dramatic
Theatre. His sister joined in and so did his mother: performances were
delivered to the family. And his elder brother began taking him to the
films. Peter Cowie tells us that the fire sequence in *Black Beauty* excited
him so much that he stayed in bed for three days with a temperature.
His grandmother went along with him. 'She was in every way my best
friend.'[31] Then the projector arrived. There were musical evenings – his
father played the piano – visits to the opera, a boyish (aged eight)
passion for Wagner, books read aloud to him.

A childhood, then, made for the director he became. Culturally
varied and testing – both the participating and the viewing/listening;

religiously resolute, as he said later, a wall to beat against; full of great certainties and the implacable Gods of Right and Wrong, Truth and Falsehood, Good and Evil; passion below the surface but suppurating and there to be picked up on the radar of the sensitive; mollycoddling both materially and quasi-maternally from a grandmother and an old cook; and accidents of location – Uppsala – and circumstance – the morgue – which can be drawn right through to *The Seventh Seal*.

There were many other experiences before he left home – the increasing knowledge of the film buff, the increasing reliance on his own company – but one, I think, above all needs attention.

In 1934 he went to Germany with two thousand other Swedish youths on an exchange. He fell in love but, also, more importantly, conceived a passion for Hitler which carried on into the war. There are many mitigating circumstances. The Swedish children were told to look up to Germany as a model. The household in which he found himself in Germany was charming and cultured. The friendships he made were warm. He was young, politically innocent, and Hitler was a huge and dramatic figure. Nevertheless, Bergman describes himself as distraught and furious with his father, his elder brother and everyone in a position to know better when he discovered, late in the war, the atrocities of the concentration camps, the hounding of the Jews, the real face of Nazism. Just as he has never denied his infatuation with Hitler, so he has made a great point of emphasising his permanent disenchantment with politics ever since.

The initial swooning towards Hitler and Nazism shows the way in which Bergman could be overwhelmed by a power figure and by drama. The connections between Hitler and his all-powerful father are clear. That photograph of his father in the pulpit returns to haunt us. It reveals in a way both the naiveté and the worrying susceptibility of the young Bergman. It is nobody's loss that he has steered clear of politics ever since, but one must add that it took him a long time to find out for himself what others of his age – late teens, even early twenties – in Europe were very soon aware of. That points either to an even deeper alliance with Hitler than he has acknowledged or, much more likely, a Bergman living in a world so much of his own, so ego-bound and trussed up in his own direct concerns and career, that even Hitler was no more than a figure on the outer rim of reality.

And soon after this visit to Germany he was strictly alone. Aged eighteen, in a classic rupture, he responded to a blow from his father by knocking the older man down. His mother intervened and she too was knocked down. Bergman fled to his bedroom and later that day left the house. He was not to see his parents for four years. Some contact was kept – gifts and the inevitable laundry! – but a severe break was made. Bergman was on his own and his career had begun, a career which could find roots and a path in one of the few European cities unblasted by war.

War surrounded him, but at a distance – like the plague to the Knight in *The Seventh Seal*. The forces of oppression and authoritarianism were implacable – like the church in *The Seventh Seal*. Sex and money were absent from Bergman's family as it is from the life of the Knight and his lady in the film. Silence – which he describes as another cruel punishment inflicted on him by his parents – the silence of God in *The Seventh Seal*. And there is much more – from the puppet theatre (the travelling stage show in the film), to the *Black Beauty* fire (the burning of the young 'witch'), to the joy and entertainment given by theatre and music – all these matters together with the overwhelming matter of the search for God's true path can be drawn from his childhood, a childhood which ended with an act of Greek passion, out of a different, pagan, hedonistic culture which also ripples the surface of *The Seventh Seal*. Bergman's race towards women, the theatre, the cinema and fame over the next years was to test to the limit his detachment from the catechism of Luther.

5

. . . .

THE MAKING OF THE FILM

Let us say that between leaving home in the late 1930s and making *The Seventh Seal* in 1957, Bergman roared to glory. In a book as brief as this it would unbalance the enterprise even to list the number of stage productions, amateur and professional, the number of radio plays, the number of film scripts written (one rewritten in four hours – and *made*), the number published, the films made, the learning gone through, the actors assembled, the sense of family – so vital to him as a man and as a director – developed.

The Seventh Seal was the seventeenth film he had directed. He had scripted six other films which were directed by others and worked on many other scripts with other writers. His stage productions, if one includes amateur productions, are too numerous to list, but he managed about three or four major productions a year from 1944 to 1956. He also wrote twenty-three stage plays, as we have said, and worked on dozens of radio plays.

His genius was early recognised. Stina Bergman (the coincidence was important to Ingmar Bergman), widow of Sweden's great playwright Hjalmar Bergman and a very influential figure at Svensk Filmindustri, read a rave review of a play by him called *The Death of Punch*. It read, 'No debut in Sweden has given such unambiguous promise for the future.' She saw him that day, hired him on the spot and put him in the documentary division. He was twenty-two.

He was living the life of a bohemian, obsessed by sex, afflicted with a temperament which provoked infidelity, veering from exultant high passion to depression – a pattern which in varying formations pursued him throughout his life. His parallel obsession was with work, although whether the work came before women or because of women is something he is anxious to question: did he, he has asked himself, begin to work in the theatre (amateur) as soon as he left home because he could meet beautiful women there? The link between the women in his life and the life in his work is as close as with Picasso. His love for Bibi Andersson wholly informs the final message, scent, tone of *The Seventh Seal* – she is Mia, the Mary, the sweet source of joy and hope and pleasure. 'Lust' is the word he prefers but it is useful to leave 'lust' for the wife of Plog in that film. The interaction of Bergman the lover, the loved person and the film is a book waiting to be written.

His bohemianism was flat out. Cigarettes galore; careless clothes; remarkable behaviour; playing the outcast to the hilt and yet smuggling his socks back to his mother for the weekly wash. A common European figure: the middle-class bohemian. But the ideas and the belief in and devotion to the work none the less valid for that. In fact one could argue that the basic security was an enabling jet: it enabled him to lift off with no more than aesthetic qualms, which is the best a young artist could hope for. And he did what he damned well pleased. No restraints from the parents; no sexless encounters; nothing but the wonderful illness of perfect licence and the great adventure of Art. He was soon a Name. Liked, and disliked, strongly. Soon married, a father, unfaithful, moved on. Children, his own, play practically no part in his conversation, and yet there were children by more than one wife.

It was by no means an uninterrupted or an undiverted ride to eminence, inevitable as it seems in retrospect. Plays were rejected; films bombed – even wonderful films (*Sawdust and Tinsel*) bombed. He had to

Bibi Andersson as Mia

fight to get his ideas accepted. Budgets were tiny, about the same (I find this an intriguing parallel) as budgets for a British television drama of the same length at the time. And then he had a break.

Smiles of a Summer Night won a major award at the Cannes Film Festival in 1956. That award waved on *The Seventh Seal*. It is a useful example of a masterpiece being given life by a prize. Until then the script of *The Seventh Seal* had been turned down emphatically.

Smiles of a Summer Night is a Mozartian comedy with even the contrasting darker shades brushed in lightly. It celebrated Bergman's joy at meeting and living with Bibi Andersson, who had a tiny part in the film. Harriet Andersson was also in it, and Eva Dahlbeck, who had given him his greatest success (in 1952) in *Waiting Women*, and Gunnar Björnstrand, who had co-starred with her. Gunnar Fischer was the lighting cameraman, as he had been and was to be on so many Bergman films until Sven Nykvist came along. There was trouble over the budget. Bergman made his typical last-minute artistic compromises which so often turned out to be artistic gains, and against all expectations the film brought him to fame in Cannes.

He has never been one for the big official occasions. *Fanny and Alexander* got four Academy Awards and he sent his current wife along to collect them. But he raced down to Cannes – with the script of *The Seventh Seal*. Svensk Filmindustri thought they were in the big time, selling *Smiles of a Summer Night* worldwide. The medieval script was now accepted – but: only thirty-five days' shooting were granted and the budget was tight, even, by contemporary standards in the UK, tiny. Bergman rushed back to Sweden, rewrote the script five times and then gathered in the troops.

Bibi Andersson would have a good part; Gunnar Björnstrand of course; and others he had worked with in the theatre, notably Bengt Ekerot and Max von Sydow. Gunnar Fischer did the photography; Erik Nordgren, as so often, did the music; Else Fisher, his first wife from way back in 1944, did the choreography. He kept to the schedule and to the budget.

It is possible to trace a very great number of cultural influences in the script and film, and Peter Cowie notes some of them: Picasso's picture of the two acrobats; Carl Orff's 'Carmina Burana'; Strindberg's *Folk Sagas* and *To Denmark*; the church frescoes which Bergman went especially to see in Haskeborga Church. Just before beginning *The Seventh Seal* he directed for radio the old *Play of Everyman* by Hugo von Hofmannstahl, in which Max von Sydow was highly praised for his 'pious emotional power'.

The budget was between 700,000 and 800,000 crowns ($150,000). There were only three days on location – principally the opening sequence and the other hillside shots. One of those was the famous Dance of Death shot, which was improvised at such short notice that one of the actors (playing the blacksmith) had a stand-in. The weather and the location and the light were perfect and Bergman grabbed it in one take.

It was a film full of improvisation. The greater part was shot in the studios at Råsunda. Bergman is delighted to tell you that in one deep-forest sequence you can, if you look hard enough, see the plate-glass windows of a block of flats, and that the stream in the forest was in fact the overflow from a loose pipe which threatened to flood the place. The great scene with the flagellants was shot in a single day – extras coming from local geriatric homes. Bergman has often described it as a time of enormous fun.

He had his film family about him. Actors from the theatre, actors he had worked with before in film, actors who seemed to him to bring a new dimension to screen acting: intelligent people acting intelligent parts seriously and well. The film was dedicated to Bibi Andersson, who was to work with him on more films and live with him, as did several of his leading actresses. 'He has two sides to his talent,' she has said, 'one intuitive, chaotic, one disciplined, certain about amounts of money and amount of days.'[32] Liv Ullman said, 'It's like being with a lover, a lover who cares, you want to give of your best.'[33] 'His background taught him to listen,' said Max von Sydow, 'and to feel and to try to find out what is going on beneath the surface.'[34]

The face and the talent of course, but the long face of Max von Sydow was undoubtedly another factor which drew so many into the film. It is a face conspicuous for its severity, but capable of serenity too. If it is possible to describe a 'thinking face', then Max von Sydow has that. There's never any doubt that he is a man questing for the knowledge of life, that ancient and too often banal enquiry which, he convinces us, has seriousness as its proper purpose. Sydow is, in many

ways, a very modern actor: his command is understated, his moments of extreme emotion are when he believes himself to be observed by no one save, perhaps, God. Sydow was to go on through many films with Bergman, as much an icon to some – the intelligent actor – as Bergman's actresses became examples for modern women. All of them became part of the family he always needed about him to do his work.

The family included the crew, of course, and there would be family treats. Every Thursday, Bergman would have a film show and often bring in the latest European films which, some of the actors have said, educated them in film acting. In his home movies or in Svensk Filmindustri movies, Bergman is often to be seen most happily at a large table with thirty or so others. There is a delightful moment from the filming of *Fanny and Alexander* when Bergman joins in the Christmas dance around the apartment. His face and actions are full of glee. Being part of the action of the actors is one of his great pleasures.

Bergman (right) directs the Actors

There are three Actors in *The Seventh Seal* and some entertaining lines on the profession. Mia is actress as a grace. She is as easy and natural about it as she is about playing with her child or welcoming the Knight. It is simply part of her life and there is no strain, no perceptible difference between the life and the art. Jof, her husband, the juggler, is the Holy Fool of an actor, from the Middle Ages which Bergman admires so much and perhaps idealises. He wants his son to do the 'one impossible trick' – make one of the juggling balls stand absolutely still in the air. Mia mocks him about this but we know he believes that it is possible. He has visions, which Bergman allows us, the audience, to see but not Mia his wife, thus siding with Jof. For Jof speaks the truth. These are not tricks or fantasies but true visions, of 'Our Lady' and later, crucially for the plot, of 'Death'. Here is the artist as magician, as one who can see into another, hidden world and bring it to light. But he suffers for this knowledge. 'You're such a damned fool,' says Skat, the

The knight is given milk and wild strawberries

older, bolder member of the three-strong troupe, 'so you're going to be the Soul of Man.' 'That's a bad part,' agrees Jof.[35]

Later, after Skat has run off with Plog the blacksmith's wife, Jof goes to the inn and is first humiliated and then all but killed, saved only by the Squire. Bergman enjoys some good cracks against actors. Plog is looking for his wife. 'Has she deserted you?' asks Jof. 'With an actor,' says Plog. 'An actor!' says Jof. 'If she's got such bad taste, then I think you should let her go.' Plog then says he will kill the actor. 'Now I understand,' says Jof. 'There are too many of them, so even if he hasn't done anything in particular, you ought to kill him merely because he's an actor.'[36] He is then revealed as an actor and tormented, made to perform tricks, baited and saved only by a miracle.

The scene following this is the most tender in the film. The Knight is given hospitality by Mia and Jof – milk and wild strawberries. It is here that the Knight comes nearest to peace and an understanding of life. In the simple serenity of just *being*, on a summer evening. Simple food, simple people. He conceives an affection for the actor and his wife and they become his purpose. Later, when he understands that Death will take them all, he creates a diversion to enable Jof and Mia and Mikael their child to slip away to safety. In that sense the actor is the Knight's grail. And Jons will, literally, save Jof's life.

There is a third actor, Skat, who is vain, philandering, overbearing, rather foolish but not without a touching courage. He is a skit on the more common notion of an actor – a self-centred and rather untrustworthy person who will even fake his own death if it is required. Plog's wife, whom he has seduced, switches back to her husband and tells him, 'He is only a false beard, false teeth, false smiles, rehearsed lines, and he's as empty as a jug. Just kill him.'[37] And Death takes him just as it spares Jof.

Bergman has spoken time and again with the deepest respect and love for the actors in his films. When we did the 'South Bank Show' film, he told me:

Sometimes a miracle is happening in front of the camera. If you are very close to the people around the camera and there is an atmosphere of confidence – real confidence – suddenly something happens in front of camera – and that is the most beautiful thing that exists. Some third dimension is present, something you can't calculate or rehearse.[38]

In *The Seventh Seal* he had actors of the highest quality, a cameraman he was still deeply satisfied with (although he was to fall out with Gunnar Fischer and take up with Sven Nykvist), a script which had begun as a play and been reworked several times – 'When I shoot the picture, I have already planned how to edit it,' he told me.[39] Above all, on that idyllic set with its little copses and open spaces out at Råsunda, he had total control. That is central to everything with Bergman. 'Like a flu, like a virus – I have to be involved – everybody in the studio has to be infected by the virus. What I want are people of high standards and integrity who like to play the game with me.'[40]

He said that he thinks of each film as his last. 'If I don't think that way, I would have some consideration – I have to sympathise to this one or be nice to that one. It's the only thing I have to be loyal to – the picture and the people around me.'[41]

The Seventh Seal would have made a fine last film.

6

. . . .

A FILM BY INGMAR BERGMAN

The credits – white on black – go through swiftly. The film begins in print. We read:

> In the middle of the fourteenth century, Antonius Block and his Squire, after long years as Crusaders in the Holy Land, have at last returned to their native Sweden, a land ravaged by the Black Plague.

The screen goes black. The music, 'Dies Irae', begins solemnly. The screen flashes light – a cloud whitened in an otherwise grey and turbulent sky. The choir burst out on the cut: a dramatic reworking of the 'Dies Irae' music. The second cut is to a solitary sea eagle hovering almost motionless against that sky. The third cut is to a barren shoreline: the music is taken out. A quiet and gentle voice reads from the Book of Revelations: 'And when the Lamb had opened the seventh seal there was silence in heaven for the space of half an hour. And the seven Angels which had the seven Trumpets prepared themselves to sound.' Two cuts have taken us closer to the action: horses in the shallows of the sea; the Knight waking, the Squire asleep. The Knight opens his eye and looks to the sky. He goes to wash in the sea. Then he prays, an intense medium close-up. As he walks from his prayers, we see the chess set, arranged. It dissolves into the sea. The waves cut out. The silence introduces Death. The dialogue begins. 'Who are you?' 'I am Death.'

Even in those few cuts there is more. We see that the chess set is laid out beside the sleeping Knight; that the Squire sleeps with a bared dagger in his hand; that the sea is cold and unrelenting, the beach stony, unyielding. When the Knight wakes, he looks challengingly, even angrily, at the sky. When he prays, his lips do not move; perhaps he can no longer pray.

After the encounter with Death, 'medieval music' gives the prod: the two men riding together along the shoreline give us the information about the plague – the encounter with the skull in the habit of a monk reintroduces the 'Dies Irae' – and we know that the two men have worn

The opening shots of the film

each other down but are welded together on their quest. They pass by a caravan. In silence, but for a horse's neigh, we come to the interior setting of the players' caravan, the three sleeping heads together inside, the idyllic encampment outside, Jof tumbling, singing, joking, talking to his horse. Everything is dappled, unthreatening, full of living.

Within those few minutes the story of the film is all foretold. The plot is fixed: the Knight will challenge Death and he will fail because Death cannot lose. The plague will accompany them on their quest but so will the grace of innocence. Strong, even primal images obtain – the sky (the Heavens), the sea (the Womb), the stony beach (the Life/Death of Man), the hovering sea eagle (the Soul of Man). Everywhere the indifference of Nature. Bergman allows you many interpretations with the simplest of techniques. Death appears as a monk, reappears as a skull in monk's clothing, will soon reappear as an actor's mask. Death is the ultimate final challenge, the final reality and yet part of our play.

The music marks each movement, with unselfconscious emphasis. The 'Dies Irae' is played over the sky which is violently featured, half blinding light, half dark, poised to usher in the Revelations of the opening of the seventh seal. A medieval dancing sound sets off the Knight and his Squire on their travels, a sound soon to be punctured by the 'Dies Irae' which punches behind the dead skull. After that the Squire's ironic and funny comments on the skull's 'most eloquent', gravedigger humour again point to another strand – the Knight's unremitting seriousness, the Squire's agnostic and wry worldliness.

The way in which Bergman lets us see the Knight and the Squire merely brush past the tiny acting troupe is masterly. The alert is given. These two stories will be intertwined, and therefore all that happens in the simple morning awakening – so contrasted with the great drama of Death and Play and Danger on the stormy beach – is given an extra resonance because we know that the story-teller has not had the Knight and the Squire pass by without a reason.

And from this beginning the whole film curves like an arc to its end when the pure-hearted players – without the rascal, Skat – escape Death; and the Knight, still seeking Knowledge of God, faces Death with the Squire remaining silent but under protest. The players go off into light; the others into darkness. The Dance of Death reaffirms the black and light contrast of that part of the film's style: simple sunlight and the mundanity of the fact of existence are all the optimism you need or are offered. Jof's visions are one individual's grace: incommunicable however significant. 'You and your visions.' Faith, a faith that sustains, is wholly individual and depends not on the Knight's knowledge but on a blessing. 'The one impossible trick.' Faith coincides with magic.

In the next scene we go to the church and meet the painter, who is another teller of the story, and the priest, who is revealed as Death. Here the Squire asserts his worldliness and the plague is underlined; here Antonius Block reaffirms his determination to live and search while there is blood in his veins. The actors constantly move out of light into dark, themes introduced at the beginning are stroked in again and again. The terrible doubt of Antonius Block is spelled out, intercut with the face of Christ on the Cross and the confessional grill behind which Death is outwitting him. 'I cry to Him in the dark but there seems to be no one there.' 'My whole life has been a meaningless search.' He looks for 'one significant action'. He will find it in saving the Holy Family. Here he rededicates himself. We then cut to the Squire who mocks God: 'Only an idealist could have thought it out.' Like Hitler? The differences between them deepen but they are bound together. The Squire sneers at his master behind his back, but he follows him.

And we walk out of the church to the tolling of the bell to meet the 'witch', the girl who has had 'carnal knowledge of the evil one'. The Knight is intrigued and compassionate; equally compassionate but angry at the brutality of it all, his Squire once again contrasts and complements his master.

On to a deserted village which Bergman presents through unemotional medium-long shots and then a mini-track which suggests something ominous and unthinkable. Here, having met the girl-witch who cries and talks, we meet the girl who is mute; having met the painter in a Christian church, we meet the fallen priest. Raval, thief, looter. The ideas are mined ever more deeply as the film moves on.

The next sequence, the performance of the Actors, gentle, too gentle for the crowd, sweet, too sweet to hold the villagers, is contrasted with the smith and his wife, he so easily betrayed, she lascivious and successful – one contrast piled on another. Skat is humiliated but then 'redeems' himself with the smith's wife in a swift and brilliant scene of seduction.

One of the characteristics of this film is the remarkable speed with which Bergman sets up and follows through each scene. It moves easily: there is no sense of strain and yet we are launched right into the heart of each new argument. For it is constructed like an argument. It is a story told as a sermon might be delivered: an allegory rooted in the opening texts, the words 'Dies Irae' and the two sentences from Revelations which recur near the very end when the Knight's lady reads them aloud and Death enters to claim them all.

When we meet the 'witch', for instance, there is not a foot of film wasted. We learn everything essential about her plight and her drama in the shortest possible time. It is an urgent film in that sense – and a highly artificial one, though such is the naturalistic persuasiveness of the medium and the great skill of the actors that there is no scene which appears merely stylised. One of the ways Bergman achieves this is to be unafraid to find ways to give basic information – on the meaning of the flagellants, for instance, who arrive seamlessly, having been 'trailed' a little earlier in the film. And once again there is no side-play: the flagellants and their spokesman go to the heart of the matter, make their point, fulfil their place in the argument and move on.

Perhaps it is this which makes *The Seventh Seal* such a satisfying film and a film which it is so easy to return to and remember: that each scene is at once so simple and so charged and layered that it catches us again and again. The pictures appear and indeed are almost elementary, the stuff of early illustrated books, of woodcuts and church paintings; the arguments too are uncomplicated, as are the characters, their nature and their journeys clearly etched out; the background of the Plague is as firmly there as, say, the foreground of Plog's muttonheaded bewilderment; the music is not unexpected and the landscape is as consistently reinforcing as the camerawork.

The Seventh Seal may not be Bergman's best film – although it is well within his top half-dozen in my opinion – but it is persistently his most referred to. And I think it is the speed of the attack which is the final trick, the speed with which he moves from scene to scene, saying all that needs to be said and then moving on, taking great issues and small alike with comparable seriousness, going for the obvious – the moment of still life when Antonius holds the milk given him by Mia, the excesses of the flagellants – mixing the sacred and the profane, the tragic and the comic with Shakespearean chemistry and doing it with such confidence. Somehow all of Bergman's own past, that of his father, that of his reading and doing and seeing, that of his Swedish culture, of his political burning and religious melancholy, poured into a series of pictures which carry that swell of contributions and contradictions so effortlessly that you could tell the story to a child, publish it as a storybook of photographs and yet know that the deepest questions of religion and the most mysterious revelation of simply being alive are both addressed. In that sense, in the sense of this film being a structure which comes out of so many converging influences in Bergman himself, in the crew, in the cast and in us as viewers, he is justified in the final sentence of his introduction to the text of the film:

> Regardless of whether I believe or not, whether I am a Christian or not, I would play my part in the collective building of the cathedral.[42]

Above: Bergman directing the flagellants
Overleaf: The Dance of Death

NOTES

· ·

1 Ingmar Bergman, *The Seventh Seal*, script (London: Lorrimer, 1968; revised ed., 1984).
2 Ibid.
3 Ibid.
4 Ibid.
5 David Jones, *Epoch and Artist* (London: Faber and Faber, 1959).
6 Bergman, *The Seventh Seal*.
7 'Bergman the Director', Thames Television, London.
8 'Ingmar Bergman' ('The South Bank Show', London, 1978).
9 Ibid.
10 Ibid.
11 Ibid.
12 Ibid.
13 *Bergman on Bergman* (London: Secker & Warburg, 1970).
14 Peter Cowie, *Ingmar Bergman* (London: Martin Secker & Warburg Limited, 1982).
15 Ibid.
16 Ibid.
17 Bergman, *The Seventh Seal*.
18 Ibid.
19 Ibid.
20 Ibid.
21 Ibid.
22 'Ingmar Bergman' ('The South Bank Show').
23 'Bergman the Director' (Thames Television).
24 Cowie, *Ingmar Bergman*.
25 Quoted in Cowie, p. 6.
26 Ibid.
27 Quoted in Cowie, p. 7.
28 *Bergman on Bergman*.
29 Ibid.
30 Ibid.
31 Ibid.
32 'Bergman the Director' (Thames Television).
33 Ibid.
34 Ibid.
35 Bergman, *The Seventh Seal*.
36 Ibid.
37 Ibid.
38 'Ingmar Bergman' ('The South Bank Show').
39 Ibid.
40 Ibid.
41 Ibid.
42 Bergman, *The Seventh Seal*.

CREDITS

The Seventh Seal (Det sjunde inseglet)

Sweden
1956
Production Company
Svensk Filmindustri
Swedish premiere
16 February 1957
UK release
13 March 1958
UK Distributor
Contemporary
Production manager
Allan Ekelund
Studio manager
Carl-Henry Cagarp
Director
Ingmar Bergman
Assistant director
Lennart Olsson
Screenplay
Ingmar Bergman from his
play *Trämalning*
**Photography (black and
white)**
Gunnar Fischer
Assistant photography
Åke Nilsson
Music
Erik Nordgren
Musical direction
Sixten Ehrling
Editor
Lennart Wallén
Art direction
P. A. Lundgren
Costumes
Manne Lindholm
Choreography
Else Fisher
Make-up
Nils Nettil
Sound
Aaby Wedin
Sound assistant
Lennart Wallin
Special sound effects
Evald Andersson

Stills
Louis Huch
95 minutes
8,600 feet

Max von Sydow
Antonius Block, the knight
Inga Landgré
Karin, the knight's wife
Gunnar Björnstrand
Jons, the squire
Nils Poppe
Jof, the jester
Bibi Andersson
Mia, the jester's wife
Bengt Ekerot
Death
Åke Fridell
Plog, the blacksmith
Inga Gill
Lisa, the blacksmith's wife
Erik Strandmark
Jonas Skat
Bertil Anderberg
Raval
Gunnel Lindblom
Mute girl
Maud Hansson
Witch
Gunnar Olsson
Church painter
Anders Ek
Monk
Lars Lind
*Young monk outside
church*
Bengt-Åke Bengtsson
Tavern keeper
Tor Borong
Peasant in tavern
Gudrun Brost
Woman in tavern
Harry Asklund
Merchant in tavern
Ulf Johansson
Leader of the soldiers

**Sten Ardenstam,
Gordon Löwenadler**
Soldiers
Karl Widh
Disabled man
Tommy Karlsson
Mikael, Jof and Mia's son
**Siv Aleros,
Bengt Gillberg,
Lars Granberg,
Gunlög Hagberg,
Gun Hammargren,
Uno Larsson,
Lennart Lilja,
Monica Lindman,
Helge Sjökvist,
Georg Skarstedt,
Ragnar Sörman,
Lennart Tollén,
Caya Wickström**
Flagellants
Ove Svensson
Corpse on hillside

With Catherine Berg,
Mona Malm, Tor Isedal,
Josef Norman,
Gösta Prüzelius,
Fritjof Tall, Nils Whiten.

The National Film Archive
print of *The Seventh Seal* was
specially acquired from
Darvill Associates.

**BFI Film Classics '. . . could scarcely be improved upon . . .
informative, intelligent, jargon-free companions.'**
The Observer

Each book in the BFI Film Classics series honours a great film from the history of world cinema – *Singin' in the Rain*, *Citizen Kane*, *Brief Encounter*, *Les enfants du paradis*. With four new titles published each spring and autumn, the series is rapidly building into a collection representing some of the best writing on film.

If you would like to receive further information about future BFI Film Classics or about other books on film, media and popular culture from BFI Publishing, please fill in your name and address and return the card to the BFI*.

No stamp is needed if posted in the UK, Channel Islands, or Isle of Man.

NAME

ADDRESS

POSTCODE

*North America: Please return your card to;
Indiana University Press, Attn: LPB, 601 N Morton Street, Bloomington, IN 47401-3797

**BFI Publishing
21 Stephen Street
FREEPOST 7
LONDON
W1E 4AN**